MAR 10 1995

j No

‖‖‖‖‖‖‖‖‖‖‖‖‖‖‖‖‖‖‖‖‖
W9-BJM-258

DISCARDED

GOOD EATING EVERY DAY

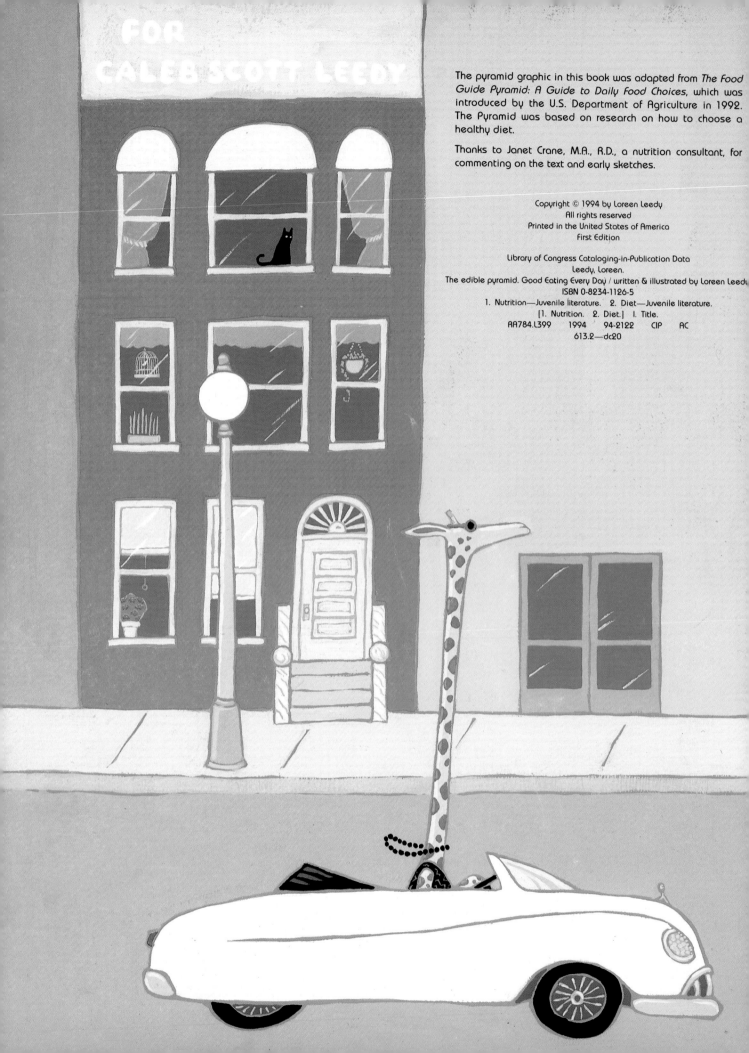

FOR
CALEB SCOTT LEEDY

The pyramid graphic in this book was adapted from *The Food Guide Pyramid: A Guide to Daily Food Choices*, which was introduced by the U.S. Department of Agriculture in 1992. The Pyramid was based on research on how to choose a healthy diet.

Thanks to Janet Crane, M.A., R.D., a nutrition consultant, for commenting on the text and early sketches.

Library of Congress Cataloging-in-Publication Data
Leedy, Loreen.
The edible pyramid. Good Eating Every Day / written & illustrated by Loreen Leedy
ISBN 0-8234-1126-5
1. Nutrition—Juvenile literature. 2. Diet—Juvenile literature.
[1. Nutrition. 2. Diet.] I. Title.
RA784.L399   1994   94-2122   CIP   AC
613.2—dc20

The Edible Pyramid

GOOD EATING

EVERY DAY

written & illustrated by

Loreen Leedy
Holiday House, New York

On the day of the grand opening of The Edible Pyramid restaurant, customers lined up to get inside.

I hope there is a salad bar.

I hope they have seafood.

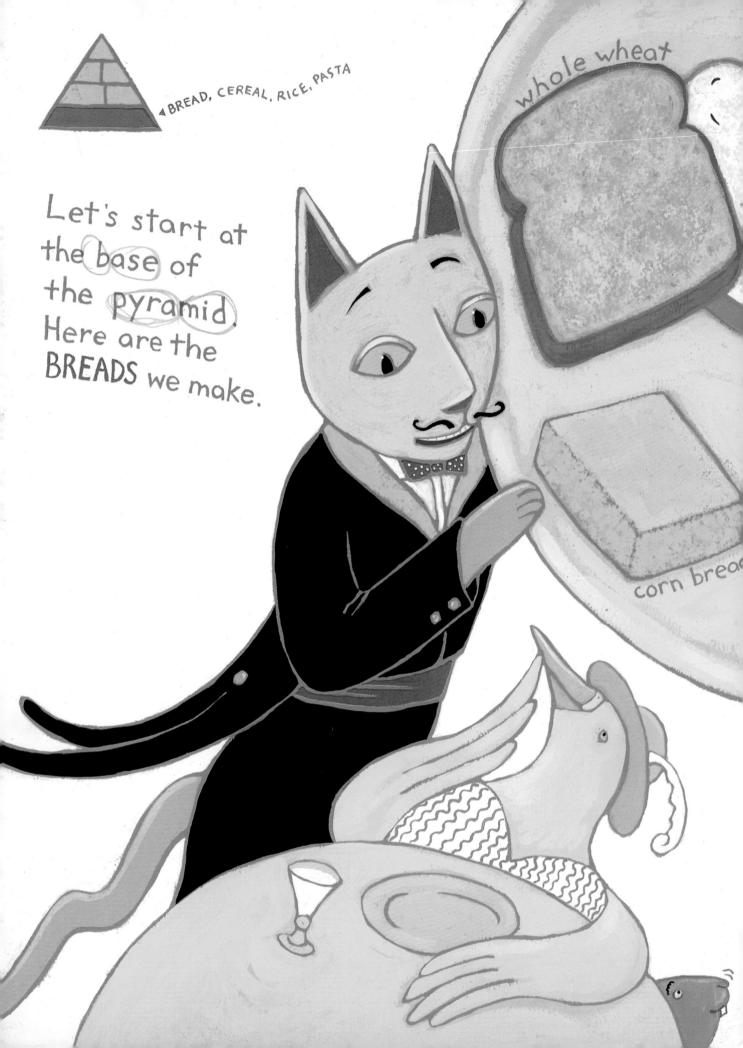

BREAD, CEREAL, RICE, PASTA

Let's start at the base of the pyramid. Here are the BREADS we make.

whole wheat

corn bread

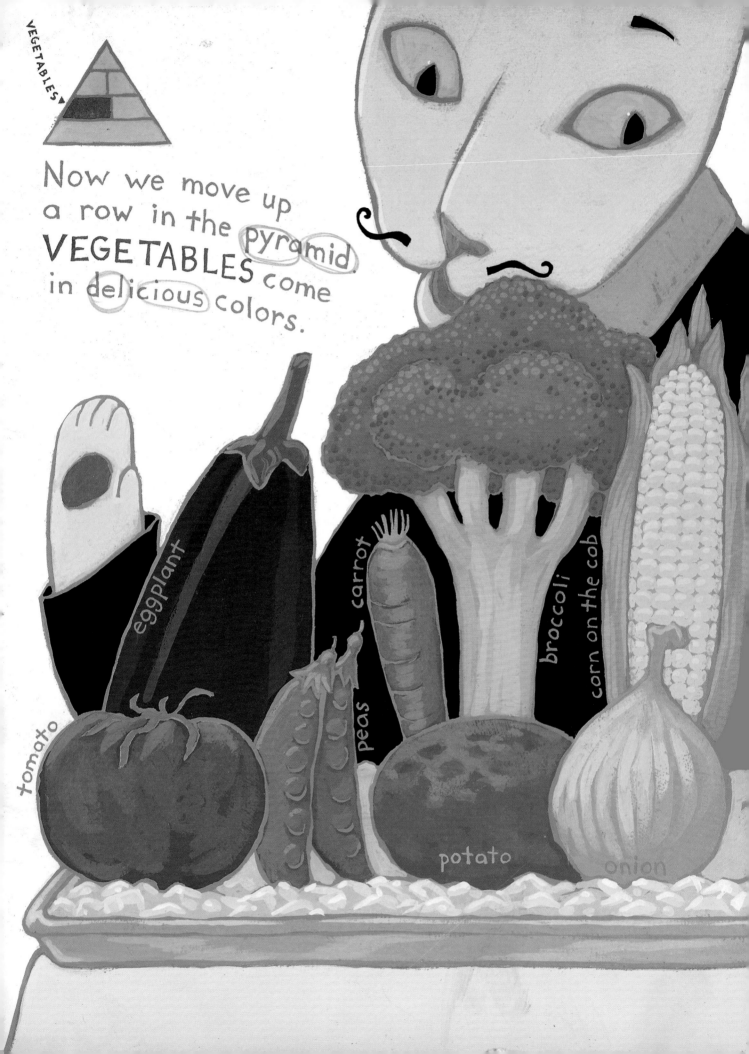

Now we move up a row in the pyramid. VEGETABLES come in delicious colors.

peach

cherry

banana

cantaloupe

apple

lemon

strawberry

MEAT, POULTRY, EGGS, FISH, DRY BEANS, NUTS

Here are just a few
of the ways we serve
MEAT, POULTRY,
FISH, and EGGS.

beefsteak

meatballs

ham

flounder

tuna

caviar
(fish eggs)

shrimp

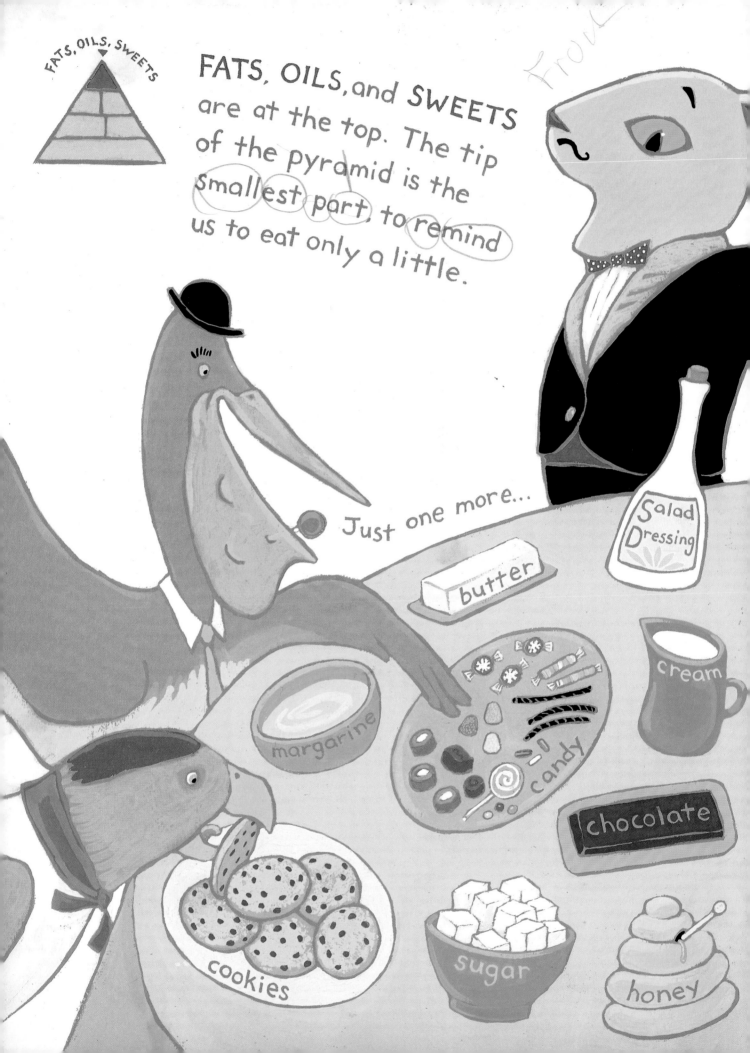

FATS, OILS, SWEETS

FATS, OILS, and SWEETS are at the top. The tip of the pyramid is the smallest part, to remind us to eat only a little.

Just one more...

Salad Dressing

butter

cream

margarine

candy

chocolate

cookies

sugar

honey

The menu says to eat 6 to 11 servings of BREAD, CEREALS, and PASTA a day. Isn't that a lot?

Let's count servings...
2 of bread,
1 of pasta, and
1 of crackers...
equals 4 servings just in this meal!

◄ 1 slice bread

◄ 1 slice bread

◄ $\frac{1}{2}$ cup pasta salad

◄ several crackers

Sometimes, foods are mixed together like in pizza. Just estimate how many servings of each food group there are.

I think everyone has plenty to eat.

Just remember to use the pyramid as a guide to which foods to eat, and how many servings every day!